The Indian in the C

L-I-T *Guide*
Literature In Teaching

By Lynne Reid Banks

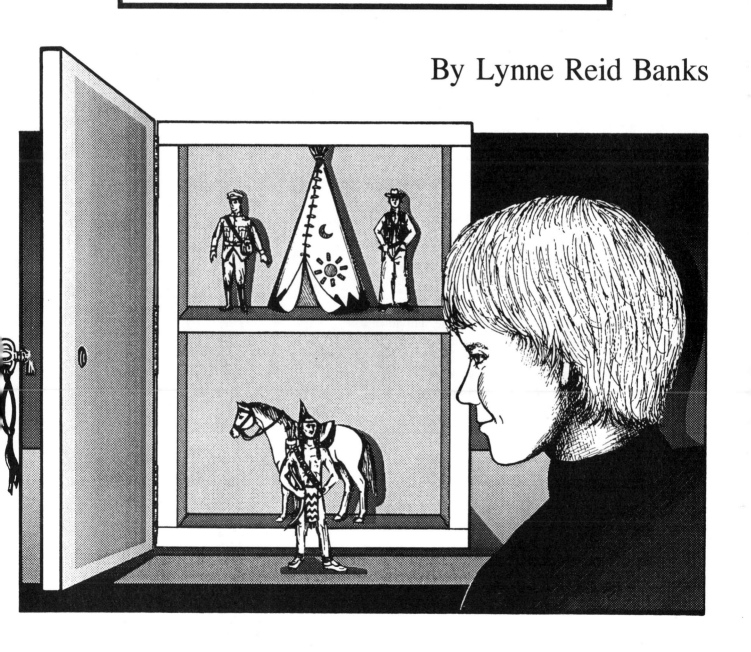

A Study Guide for Grades 3 to 7

Prepared by Charlotte S. Jaffe and Barbara T. Doherty
Illustrated by Karen Sigler

ISBN 1-56644-001-7

© 1996 Educational Impressions, Inc., Hawthorne, NJ

EDUCATIONAL IMPRESSIONS, INC.
Hawthorne, NJ 07507

Printed in the United States of America.

This study guide is based on the book *The Indian in the Cupboard:*
  Copyright 1980 by Lynne Reid Banks
  Published by Doubleday & Company, Inc.: New York.

The Indian in the Cupboard
Written by Lynne Reid Banks

STORY SUMMARY

In this fantasy, a young boy named Omri accidentally brings to life a plastic figurine. The combination of a discarded medicine cabinet and a family-heirloom key work the incredible magic.

Omri has mixed feelings about the miniature friend he has created, an Iroquois named Little Bear. Supplying food and shelter for this tiny person becomes quite an endeavor. Providing medical care is even more of a challenge!

Omri has two brothers, but he does not confide in them about his spectacular discovery. He does, however, confide in his best friend, Patrick. Patrick becomes part of the conspiracy. In fact, he insists on bringing to life a figurine of his own. Omri objects, but when Patrick is alone with the cabinet and the plastic figures, he brings to life a cowboy named Boone and his horse. The two boys and their miniature friends have interesting adventures. At the same time, they learn a great deal about relationships, prejudices, and responsibilities.

In spite of his fondness for his tiny friends, Omri realizes that they must be returned to their original existence. Of course, the cupboard and the key still exist, leading readers to believe that other adventures will follow!

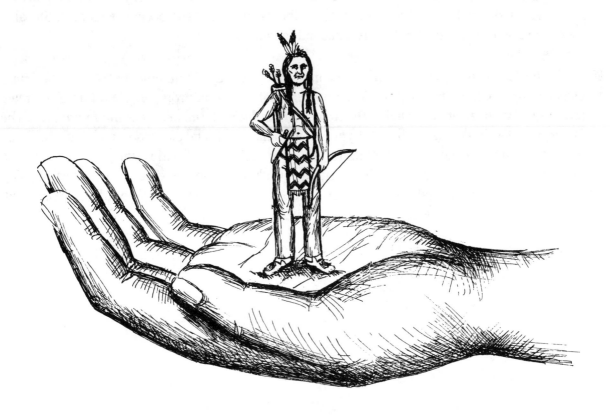

Meet the Author
Lynne Reid Banks

Prolific and award-winning author Lynne Reid Banks began life in London, England, on July 31, 1929. Her father, James Reid, was a doctor; her mother, Muriel Alexander, was a successful stage actress. During the London bombings of World War II, Lynne and her mother were evacuated to Canada, where they remained for five years. Upon her return to England, Lynne was fifteen and devastated by what she saw. "I found my city in ruins and learned what had happened there. I felt like a deserter," the author said, recalling how she had felt as an impressionable teenager.

Lynne prepared for a career as an actress at the Italia Conti Stage School and the Royal Academy of Dramatic Arts in London. Not realizing the success she had hoped for as an actress, she found employment in the television industry as a writer and reporter. She also wrote plays which were produced for the stage, radio, and television. Her first novel, *The L-Shaped Room,* was a literary success; it became a motion picture in 1962 and starred Leslie Caron. In 1960, the author fulfilled a lifelong dream and traveled to Israel, where she worked in a kibbutz, married, and became a mother. She also spent time there teaching English as a second language.

The Indian in the Cupboard received numerous awards, including the *New York Times* Outstanding Book Award in 1981. The popularity of this book prompted Reid Banks to create three equally imaginative sequels: *The Return of the Indian, The Secret of the Indian,* and *The Mystery of the Cupboard.* Although Lynne Reid Banks has found success in creating books and plays for adult audiences, she prefers to write for children. "Writing for young people is a much pleasanter and easier thing than writing for adults," she has stated. "I especially enjoy writing wish-fulfillment tales for younger children in which real, everyday life co-exists with magic."

The author resides in England with her husband, Chaim, who is a sculptor. They have three children: Adiel, Gillon, and Omri.

Pre-Reading Information
The Iroquois

The Iroquois settled in the Northeast Woodlands. Most lived in what is now the northern region of New York State. Life for the Iroquois centered around farming; therefore, their villages were rather permanent. The people lived in large bark longhouses. Families of the same clan lived together. When a man married, he became a member of his wife's clan and he moved into her family's longhouse. Each family had its own bunk and storage cell. A row of cooking fires ran down the center aisle. Each fire was shared by two families. Holes in the roof allowed the smoke to escape.

Life for the Iroquois was regulated by the seasons. In the spring the men cleared the land, and the women planted the seeds. Corn, beans, and squash, often called the Three Sisters, were the main crops. They were tended during the summer and harvested in the fall. A good harvest was important so that enough could be stored for the long winter months. Corn was the most important of all. The women shelled the corn and ground it in large wooden mortars.

Although the Iroquois were farmers, the men added to their food supply by hunting deer and other animals. They were among the few North American tribes to use a blowgun. Of course, they hunted with bows and arrows as well. Hunting was important not only as a source of food, but also for the skin, bone, and horn. The Iroquois used the skins to make their clothing. They used the bone and horn to make their combs, tools, and other utensils.

The men wore a breechclout and leggings. A breechclout was a strip of leather that hung over a belt in front and in back. Iroquois leggings were loose fitting and had embroidered seams. Women wore skirts, leggings, and sometimes capes. Both men and women wore soft-soled moccasins, often beautifully decorated.

The Iroquois were great warriors. For a long time the different tribes battled each other as well as the neighboring Algonquins. Then, around the year 1570, five of the tribes were united into the League of the Great Peace. The five tribes were the Senecas, the Onondagas, the Cayugas, the Oneidas, and the Mohawks. In 1722 the Tuscaroras also joined the confederacy. For many years these tribes did not fight each other.

The Iroquois made beads from hard clam, or quahog, shells. The shells were mostly white with some purple. Because there was less purple, the purple shells became more valuable. Called wampum, these beads were put on strings and used almost like money. Some were woven into belts. The designs on them recorded messages and events, such as treaties.

Like other Woodland Indians, the Iroquois enjoyed many games. Lacrosse was very popular with the Iroquois. The game was later adopted by the white settlers who watched the Iroquois and some of the tribes of the Southeast play the game.

Today the headquarters of the Iroquois Confederation is located on the Onondaga Reservation near Syracuse, New York.

Vocabulary
Chapter One: *Birthday Presents*

Use your dictionary to define the following words as they were used in the chapter.

1. accuse

2. appreciate

3. baffled

4. bandolier

5. cautiously

6. coherent

7. compost

8. extraordinary

9. ferociously

10. intricate

11. marvelous

12. miniscule

13. occasionally

14. secondhand

15. urged

Thank You!

It is always polite to write a thank-you note when you receive a gift. In this chapter, Omri received some special gifts for his birthday. Pretend that you are Omri. Choose one of the gifts and write a thank-you note to the giver. Use at least five vocabulary words from the first part of this activity in your letter.

Dear _____,

Comprehension and Discussion Questions
Chapter One: *Birthday Presents*

Answer the following questions in complete sentence form. Give examples from the story to support your response.

1. Why was Omri's birthday a disappointment for him?

_____

_____

_____

_____

2. Describe Omri's reaction to Gillon's surprise gift. Would you have had the same reaction? Explain.

_____

_____

_____

_____

3. Why didn't Omri tell anyone in his family that the Indian had come alive? Do you think he made the right decision? What would you have done in his place?

_____

_____

_____

_____

4. What was Omri's response when the Indian said, "You touch—I kill"? Evaluate this response.

_____

_____

_____

_____

Vocabulary
Chapter Two: *The Door Is Shut*

Use the words in the box to complete the sentences. You may need to use your dictionary.

apparently	astonished	crestfallen	dignified	eagerly
excessive	kernel	knelt	ravenously	row
strewn	suspicious	temptation	tenderly	writhed

1. The customer complained that the charges were _____.

2. Bobby couldn't resist the _____ to eat his mother's freshly baked cookies.

3. The knight _____ before the king to receive his honors.

4. Omri looked _____ when his plastic toy came to life.

5. After the long hike, the campers ate their dinner _____.

6. In Carrie's messy room, her clothes were _____ all over the floor.

7. The students _____ awaited the results of the annual Field Day Contest.

8. Michael was _____ when he learned that he had failed the history exam.

9. The new mother glanced _____ at her baby.

10. The water stain was _____ caused by a leak in the roof.

11. As we watched the king walk by, we noticed his _____ manner.

12. Our dog Prince is _____ of strangers and often growls at them.

13. The _____ of corn looked quite large and strange to the tiny Indian.

14. Amy _____ in pain when she broke her ankle during the soccer game.

15. There was a _____ at the store because two shoppers wanted the same item.

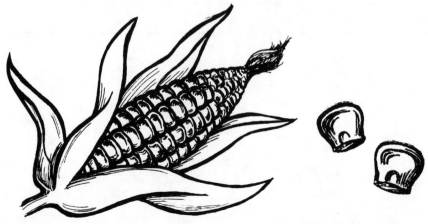

Comprehension and Discussion Questions
Chapter Two: *The Door Is Shut*

Answer the following questions in complete sentence form. Give examples from the story to support your response.

1. In what ways did Omri's behavior seem strange to Patrick on the day after his birthday?

_____

_____

_____

_____

2. Why did Omri feel the pain of sadness and disappointment. How did he unknowingly remedy this situation?

_____

_____

_____

_____

3. How did Omri react to Little Bear's demands? Do you think that having Little Bear was worth all the extra trouble? Explain your viewpoint.

_____

_____

_____

_____

4. Explain the reason that Omri would not let Little Bear remain in the cupboard.

_____

_____

_____

_____

Vocabulary
Chapter Three: *Thirty Scalps*

Match the vocabulary words on the left to the definitions on the right. Place the correct letter on each line.

_____ 1. armor   A. narrow, deep, steep-sided opening in earth's surface

_____ 2. canyon   B. indecision; pause

_____ 3. cavalry   C. extreme in degree or strength

_____ 4. despised   D. easily bent; supple

_____ 5. haunches   E. flat or rolling grassland with few trees

_____ 6. hesitation   F. defensive covering

_____ 7. intense   G. on time; without delay

_____ 8. lithe   H. foot rings hung from a saddle

_____ 9. prairie   I. to take possession by force

_____ 10. promptly   J. hindquarters of an animal

_____ 11. ransack   K. resistance to change of position

_____ 12. seize   L. soldiers who fight on horseback

_____ 13. stability   M. took a risk; dared

_____ 14. stirrups   N. hated

_____ 15. ventured   O. to search thoroughly

An **antonym** is a word that has a meaning opposite to that of another word. Choose five vocabulary words from the first part of this activity. Write an antonym for each.

_____

_____

_____

_____

_____

_____

Comprehension and Discussion Questions
Chapter Three: *Thirty Scalps*

Answer the following questions in complete sentence form. Give examples from the story to support your response.

1. What caused Omri to shout, "It's real magic, don't you understand? Magic"? Contrast Omri's reaction to Little Bear's reaction to the same magical happening.

_____

_____

_____

_____

2. Why, do you think, did Little Bear allow Omri to place him in his palm and transfer him to another location?

_____

_____

_____

_____

3. Discuss the shocking discovery that Omri made about Little Bear. How did he try to justify it? How would you have felt about Little Bear if you had been Omri?

_____

_____

_____

_____

4. Why was Omri reluctant to allow Little Bear and the horse to go outdoors?

_____

_____

_____

_____

Vocabulary
Chapters Four and Five:
The Great Outdoors and *Tommy*

For each sentence circle the most appropriate definition for the word printed in bold as it is used in the sentence. Use your dictionary to help you. The first has been done for you.

1. They were **reluctant** to cross the rickety bridge.

     happy   (unwilling)   careful

2. My **ancestors** came to America from Europe many years ago.

     relatives   acquaintances   neighbors

3. The steep **escarpment** faced the ocean.

     mountain   cliff   gorge

4. We found Bill's dog **cowering** in the corner after it was scolded.

     cringing   whining   barking

5. Mother must **cope** with the demands of caring for a new baby.

     deal   disagree   sympathize

6. Samantha wore her new blue **parka** all through the winter.

     muffler   scarf   jacket

7. The workers quickly applied a **tournequet** to his injured leg.

     bandage   medication   brace

8. The lawyer had **absolute** proof that the witness was lying.

     some   little   positive

9. Some students began to **panic** when the teacher announced a surprise quiz.

     become annoyed   show fear   argue loudly

10. During a science demonstration, I broke a **beaker**.

     narrow tube   widemouthed vessel   large dish

11. That math problem was so **complicated,** it took an hour to solve it.

     complex   long   incomplete

12. Our puppy felt sad and **forlorn** when we left him home alone.

     angry   content   abandoned

Comprehension and Discussion Questions
Chapters Four and Five

Answer the following questions in complete sentence form. Give examples from the story to support your response.

CHAPTER FOUR: *The Great Outdoors*

1. How did Little Bear's injury occur? Could it have been prevented? Explain.

_____

_____

_____

_____

2. What desperate remedy was Omri forced to take in order to help Little Bear? Predict its effectiveness.

_____

_____

_____

_____

CHAPTER FIVE: *Tommy*

1. How did Omri calm the medical orderly's initial fears? Do you think it was right for Omri to use the soldier to help Little Bear? Give reasons to support your point of view.

_____

_____

_____

_____

2. Omri decided to change Tommy back to plastic again because "it was too complicated." Do you think he made a wise decision? Explain.

_____

_____

_____

_____

Vocabulary
Chapter Six: *The Chief Is Dead, Long Live the Chief*

Use the vocabulary words in the box to create ten original sentences. When you have finished, rewrite the sentences, replacing each vocabulary word with a blank line. Only one vocabulary word should fit appropriately into each blank. You may use your dictionary. Exchange your missing-word sentences with a classmate to solve.

EXAMPLE: An important staple of the Iroquois diet was _____.
ANSWER: maize

confirmed	courtesies	crosspieces	dignity	dreamier
expelled	fascination	headdress	hectoring	patience
pry	reassure	thong	tomahawk	ungrateful

Fill in the Blanks!

Sentences Created By: _____

Sentences Filled In By: _____

1.

2.

3.

4.

5.

6.

7.

8.

9.

10.

Comprehension and Discussion Questions
Chapter Six: *The Chief Is Dead, Long Live the Chief*

Answer the following questions in complete sentence form. Give examples from the story to support your response.

1. Why was Omri so motivated to read?

_____

_____

_____

_____

2. Explain the meaning of The Three Sisters.

_____

_____

_____

_____

3. Why was it so difficult for Omri to treat the Indian chief in the same way that he had treated the knight?

_____

_____

_____

_____

4. Judge Little Bear's behavior toward the dead chief.

_____

_____

_____

_____

Vocabulary
Chapter Seven: *Uninvited Brothers*

A **synonym** is a word that has a meaning similar to that of another word. An **antonym** is a word that has a meaning opposite to that of another word. For each vocabulary word on the left write either a synonym or an antonym. You may use your dictionary.

VOCABULARY WORD	*Synonym*	*Antonym*
1. admiration		
2. burden		
3. chaos		
4. compromise		
5. engulf		
6. feeble		
7. galvanize		
8. goggle		
9. incredulous		
10. magnanimous		
11. mocking		
12. reverently		
13. soberly		
14. spirituous		
15. uncanny		

Friendship

Taking into account the importance of his friendship with Patrick, Omri finally decided to confide the secret of the Indian and the magic cupboard. Tell about a friendship that is very valuable to you. Use at least five vocabulary words from the first part of this activity.

Comprehension and Discussion Questions
Chapter Seven: *Uninvited Brothers*

Answer the following questions in complete sentence form. Give examples from the story to support your response.

1. Why did Omri finally decide to share his secret with Patrick?

_____

_____

_____

_____

2. What mistaken assumption did Omri make when he saw his brothers in his room? How did he try to prevent them from learning the truth when they heard the whinny?

_____

_____

_____

_____

3. Evaluate Patrick's statement and Omri's response: ''Maybe this isn't such fun as I thought.'' ''No, it's not *fun.*''

_____

_____

_____

_____

4. Re-read the last paragraph in Chapter Seven. Predict what might happen in the next chapter.

_____

_____

_____

_____

Vocabulary
Chapter Eight: *Cowboy!*

Read each clue and find the answers in the box. Then use the letters above the numbered spaces to decipher the secret message.

abrupt	aghast	buckskin	doggedly	dune
embedded	enormous	heron	index	infinite
instinctive	mulish	savory	spellbound	

1. persistently

___ ___ ___ ___ ___ ___ ___
1   3

2. huge

___ ___ ___ ___ ___ ___ ___
  2   27

3. a wading bird

___ ___ ___ ___ ___
  7 4

4. leather from male deer

___ ___ ___ ___ ___ ___ ___ ___
6   9

5. fascinated

___ ___ ___ ___ ___ ___ ___
    8   25

6. pleasing in taste and smell

___ ___ ___ ___ ___ ___
  11 20

7. hill or ridge of sand

___ ___ ___ ___
    10

8. endless

___ ___ ___ ___ ___ ___ ___ ___
13   14   12

9. stubborn

___ ___ ___ ___ ___ ___
15

10. struck by shock or horror

___ ___ ___ ___ ___ ___
  17 16

11. finger next to thumb

___ ___ ___ ___ ___
18

12. spontaneous; not learned

___ ___ ___ ___ ___ ___ ___ ___ ___ ___ ___
23   19

13. fixed firmly in something

___ ___ ___ ___ ___ ___ ___ ___
  21 26   24

14. unexpectedly sudden

___ ___ ___ ___ ___ ___
  22 5

1 2   3 4 5   6 7 8 9 10 11 12   13 14

___ ___ ___ ___ ___ ___ ___ ___ ___ ___ ___ ___ ___ ___

15 16 17 18 19   20 21 22 23   24 25 26 27

___ ___ ___ ___ ___ **?** ___ ___ ___ ___ ___ ___ ___ ___ **.**

Comprehension and Discussion Questions
Chapter Eight: *Cowboy!*

Answer the following questions in complete sentence form. Give examples from the story to support your response.

1. What caused Omri and Patrick to fight with each other? Whose side would you take? Explain.

_____

_____

_____

_____

2. Why did Omri leave Patrick alone in his bedroom? Why was this action a mistake?

_____

_____

_____

_____

3. Little Bear wanted Omri to act like his mother. Explain.

_____

_____

_____

_____

4. Why did Omri agree to bring the little people to school?

_____

_____

_____

_____

Vocabulary
Chapter Nine: *Shooting Match*

Use the words in the box to complete the sentences. You may need to use your dictionary.

coaxed	delirium	dolefully	frenzied
gleeful	infuriated	makeshift	mime
offended	peered	prostrate	relish
scornfully	tactics	tarnation	tethered	varmint

1. The constant teasing _____ Linda and she expressed her anger.

2. John felt contempt for the criminals and spoke of them _____.

3. Because it was _____, the dog could not reach the shade.

4. The coach _____ us into agreeing to another practice session.

5. The _____ pace of the holidays made everyone tense.

6. _____ for winning the contest were planned by each entrant.

7. Jerry was _____ by his friends' distrust, but he didn't show his hurt feelings.

8. Kate could not see them when she _____ through the window.

9. The concert of joyful songs gave us a _____ feeling.

10. Although built by inexperienced amateurs, the cabin was not at all _____.

11. Marie did not _____ the idea of working in the extreme heat.

12. The man lacked the strength to go on; he lay _____ on the ground.

13. The sheriff ran the _____ out of town.

14. The _____ acted out the skit by using gestures and body movement.

Three of the vocabulary words from the first part of this activity were not used. Write an original sentence using each of those words.

_____

_____

_____

_____

_____

Comprehension and Discussion Questions
Chapter Nine: *Shooting Match*

Answer the following questions in complete sentence form. Give examples from the story to support your response.

1. Explain what the cowboy meant when he said, " 'Why couldn't Ah see pink elly-fants and dancin' rats...other fellas see when they gits far gone?' "

_____

_____

_____

_____

2. What brought the cowboy and Little Bear together?

_____

_____

_____

_____

3. How did Omri persuade Little Bear not to harm the cowboy?

_____

_____

_____

_____

4. Boone had a nickname. What was it and how did he get it?

_____

_____

_____

_____

Vocabulary
Chapter Ten: *Breakfast Truce*

Use your dictionary to define the following words as they were used in the chapter.

1. clambered

2. clod

3. draw

4. gesture

5. hacked

6. no-holds-barred

7. nonplused

8. pummeling

9. retorted

10. scowled

11. sidled

12. truce

13. vittles

14. wisp

Create a Word Search!

Use the vocabulary words from the first part of this activity to create a word-search puzzle and exchange puzzles with your classmates.

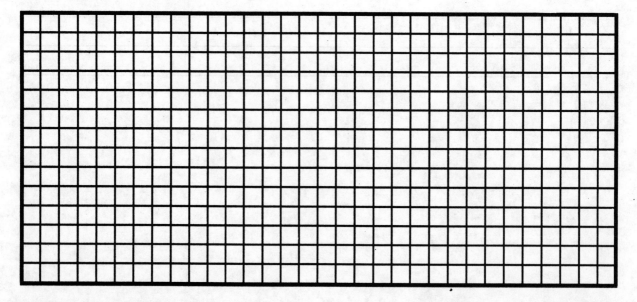

Comprehension and Discussion Questions
Chapter Ten: *Breakfast Truce*

Answer the following questions in complete sentence form. Give examples from the story to support your response.

1. Describe Omri's tactics for getting Boone and Little Bear to declare a truce.

_____

_____

_____

_____

2. What do you think of Omri's cooking skills? How did Little Bear and Boone seem to feel about them?

_____

_____

_____

_____

3. Why did Boone eat so much and so slowly?

_____

_____

_____

_____

4. Why did Omri break up the fight when he did?

_____

_____

_____

_____

Vocabulary
Chapter Eleven: *School*

Match the vocabulary words on the left to the definitions on the right. Place the correct letter on each line.

_____ 1. agony	A. inclined to be troubled
_____ 2. apprehension	B. a look of disgust or pain
_____ 3. barge	C. carefully; cautiously
_____ 4. butt	D. to enter rudely; to intrude
_____ 5. dicey	E. uneasy anticipation
_____ 6. drastic	F. bare; grim
_____ 7. fiendish	G. to care for the appearance of
_____ 8. fretful	H. to hit against with the head
_____ 9. gingerly	I. radical; severe
_____ 10. grimace	J. English game of ninepins
_____ 11. groom	K. wicked; cruel
_____ 12. musingly	L. to tease; to mock
_____ 13. raucous	M. suffering; distress
_____ 14. skittles	N. sarcastic
_____ 15. snide	O. rough-sounding; disorderly
_____ 16. stark	P. involving danger or risk
_____ 17. taunt	Q. thoughtfully

Word Categories

After you have matched the vocabulary words with their meanings, place the words into as many different categories, or groups, as possible. Give each category a title. You may use a word in more than one category. At least two words are needed to compose a group. Two examples have been started for you.

VERBS
taunt
barge

5-LETTER WORDS
barge
taunt

Comprehension and Discussion Questions
Chapter Eleven: *School*

Answer the following questions in complete sentence form. Give examples from the story to support your response.

1. What reason did Boone give for not washing his clothes?

_____

_____

_____

_____

2. Compare Omri's morning routine to your own.

_____

_____

_____

_____

3. While at school, Little Bear made a surprising request of Omri. What was it?

_____

_____

_____

_____

4. This chapter ended with Omri putting Little Bear and Boone together in his pocket and warning them not to make any noise. Predict what might happen.

_____

_____

_____

_____

Vocabulary
Chapter Twelve: *Trouble with Authority*

Choose the word in each set that is **most like** the first word in meaning. Circle that word.

1. **anticipation:**   expectation   suspicion   reunion

2. **apt:**   inclined   unsuited   gradually

3. **apparatus:**   mechanics   design   equipment

4. **bash:**   strike   shy   conceited

5. **clenched:**   muffled   loosened   closed

6. **dithered:**   diminished   hesitated   focused

7. **fragrant:**   scented   fracas   frazzle

8. **frantically:**   casually   nervously   determinedly

9. **gesticulate:**   gesture   guess   estimate

In the first part of this activity you had to look for synonyms of the vocabulary words. Now use your dictionary to find synonyms for these vocabulary words.

1. headmaster

2. hysterical

3. inquire

4. loomed

5. sulkily

6. tousled

7. ultimate

8. uneventful

Comprehension and Discussion Questions
Chapter Twelve: *Trouble with Authority*

Answer the following questions in complete sentence form. Give examples from the story to support your response.

1. Evaluate Patrick's demand that Omri immediately give Little Bear and Boone to him in the lunch line.

_____

_____

_____

_____

2. Explain the following: "he clamped down on his imagination."

_____

_____

_____

_____

3. How did the way in which Omri cared for Little Bear differ from the way in which Patrick cared for Boone?

_____

_____

_____

_____

4. Explain why Omri concluded that Patrick had shown Mr. Johnson the little men. Guess whether or not the boys will be punished. Explain why you believe as you do.

_____

_____

_____

_____

Vocabulary
Chapter Thirteen: *Art and Accusation*

Use your dictionary to define the following words as they were used in the chapter.

1. **bafflement**

2. **boasting**

3. **clamored**

4. **enthralled**

5. **flummoxed**

6. **infinitesimal**

7. **intrigued**

8. **microscopic**

9. **obliged**

10. **pounds**

11. **reckoned**

12. **staunchly**

13. **stifle**

14. **tottered**

15. **verge**

16. **vouch**

Point of View

Judge the way in which Omri was treated by the shopkeeper. Can you see both sides of the issue? Choose a point of view and write a paragraph explaining whether or not Omri was treated fairly. Use at least five vocabulary words from the first part of this activity.

_____

_____

_____

_____

_____

_____

_____

Comprehension and Discussion Questions
Chapter Thirteen: *Art and Accusation*

Answer the following questions in complete sentence form. Give examples from the story to support your response.

1. How did Omri feel about Little Bear having a wife?

_____

_____

_____

_____

2. What surprise did Omri learn about Boone while in school?

_____

_____

_____

_____

3. Evaluate the title of this chapter.

_____

_____

_____

_____

4. How was the friendship between Omri and Patrick healed?

_____

_____

_____

_____

Vocabulary
Chapter Fourteen: *The Missing Key*

Use your dictionary to define the following words as they were used in the chapter.

1. **alighted**

2. **astride**

3. **awry**

4. **chasm**

5. **gravitated**

6. **myriad**

7. **oddment**

8. **rapture**

9. **restive**

10. **sieve**

11. **shambles**

12. **smirk**

13. **tauntingly**

14. **transfixed**

15. **trowel**

Vocabulary Charade Game

Divide the class into two or more teams. Create VOCABULARY CHARADE CARDS with the word on one side and the definition on the other. The game begins when a player from one team selects a card. That player then acts out the word for his or her teammates, who have two minutes to correctly guess the word and define it. Teams alternate until all players have had a chance to act out a word or until all the words have been used. Each correct answer is worth one point.

© 1996 Educational Impressions, Inc.

Comprehension and Discussion Questions
Chapter Fourteen: *The Missing Key*

Answer the following questions in complete sentence form. Give examples from the story to support your response.

1. Why did Omri want to "bash in" Adiel?

_____

_____

_____

_____

2. What did Omri fear most about the lost key?

_____

_____

_____

_____

3. Omri hesitated to ask his mom if she'd found the key? Why?

_____

_____

_____

_____

4. Do you think Little Bear regretted shooting Boone with his arrow? Explain.

_____

_____

_____

_____

Vocabulary
Chapter Fifteen: *Underfloor Adventure*

Match the vocabulary words on the left to the definitions on the right. Place the correct letter on each line.

_____ 1. bedraggled

_____ 2. crafty

_____ 3. detect

_____ 4. eerie

_____ 5. gnawing

_____ 6. pallet

_____ 7. perils

_____ 8. prey

_____ 9. prowling

_____ 10. septic

_____ 11. superstitious

_____ 12. vulnerable

A. attackable; susceptible to injury

B. narrow, hard bed

C. infected

D. inclined to have irrational beliefs

E. to perceive

F. looking for prey

G. inspiring fear or uneasiness

H. wet and limp; shabby

I. biting; chewing

J. animal hunted for food; a victim

K. deceitful; devious

L. imminent dangers

Word Webs

Using the vocabulary words that you defined in the first part of this activity, build word webs. Place one vocabulary word in each circle. Then fill in the blanks with words that are related to the center word. Stretch your mind to think of unusual connections. An example has been done for you.

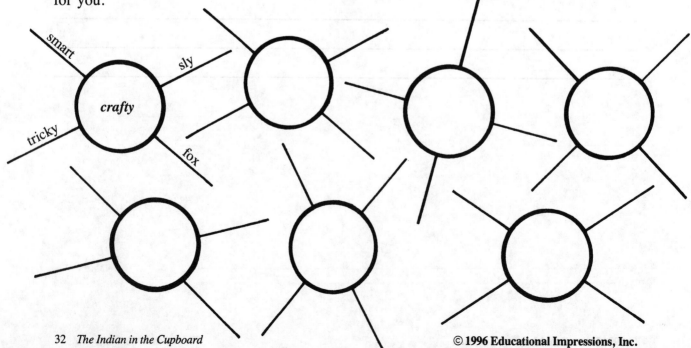

Comprehension and Discussion Questions
Chapter Fifteen: *Underfloor Adventure*

Answer the following questions in complete sentence form. Give examples from the story to support your response.

1. Why did Little Bear go under the floor? Why did Omri call him to return?

_____

_____

_____

_____

2. Why didn't the medical orderly suggest using penicillin or other antibiotics for Boone?

_____

_____

_____

3. How do we know that Little Bear's feelings about Boone had changed?

_____

_____

_____

4. What caused Little Bear to lose his temper?

_____

_____

_____

Comprehension and Discussion Questions
Chapter Sixteen: *Brothers*

Use the words in the box to complete the sentences. You may need to use your dictionary.

bewildered	bore	chanting	critter	fate
flourish	lingered	nick	pommel	ration
relapse	stealthily	stressful	swabbed	swig

1. Jane was _____ despite all the clues and directions.

2. We _____ in the garden; it was so pleasant that we didn't want to leave.

3. Being a police officer is a very _____ occupation.

4. The President signed the bill with a _____.

5. Bill was released from the hospital too quickly and had a _____.

6. Barbara fell off the horse because the _____ was missing from the saddle.

7. We heard the monks _____ each morning and evening.

8. The boys went _____ through the woods; they didn't want to be noticed.

9. When the hatchet fell, it put a _____ in the wooden floor.

10. Knowing one's _____ may not always be a good thing.

11. The nurse _____ the ointment on the patient's wound.

Four of the vocabulary words were not used in the first part of this activity. Use each of those words in an original sentence.

_____

_____

_____

_____

_____

_____

Comprehension and Discussion Questions
Chapter Sixteen: *Brothers*

Answer the following questions in complete sentence form. Give examples from the story to support your response.

1. What kept Omri awake?

_____

_____

_____

_____

2. Judge Omri's advice to Little Bear not to tell the girl about him.

_____

_____

_____

_____

3. Describe the special farewell between Omri and Little Bear.

_____

_____

_____

_____

4. What did Omri have as a souvenir?

_____

_____

_____

_____

Spotlight Literary Skill
Compare and Contrast

In your readings, you often will notice similarities and differences among characters, settings, and events. Sometimes you will be asked to compare and contrast; in other words, you will be asked to examine the likenesses and differences of two or more people, places, ideas, or things. **Contrast** always emphasizes differences. **Compare** may focus on likenesses alone or on likenesses and differences.

In this activity, you are challenged to compare and contrast characters from *The Indian in the Cupboard.*

1. Compare Omri and Patrick. In what ways are they the same?

2. Contrast Omri and Patrick. In what ways are they different?

3. Compare Little Bear and Boone. In what ways are they the same?

4. Contrast Little Bear and Boone. In what ways are they different?

Extra Challenge!

Put your findings in the form of a Venn diagram. A **Venn diagram** uses circles or ellipses to represent relations between sets. Choose either set of characters you compared and contrasted above. List their differences on the outer parts of the circles. List their similarities in the center. Write each character's name above the appropriate section of the diagram.

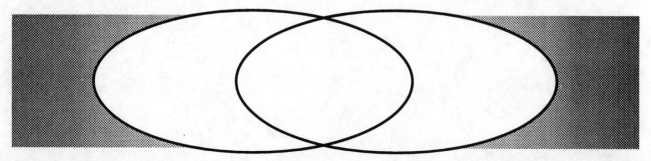

Spotlight Literary Skill
Making Conversation: Dialogue

Dialogue, the spoken words of the characters, is an important feature of most types of writing. Through dialogue we learn more about how each character thinks, feels, and relates to others. The use of dialogue allows the readers to feel present at the scene of the action.

There are many good examples of realistic dialogue in *The Indian and the Cupboard.* Write five of your favorites. For each, explain the circumstances.

1. _____
_____

2. _____
_____

3. _____
_____

4. _____
_____

5. _____
_____

Group Activity

Create an imaginary dialogue that might have taken place among several characters in the story. Remember that the characters speak English in different ways. Boone has a Texas drawl; Little Bear speaks in what Omri considers to be "Indian English"; and Omri and his friends and family speak British English. Try to keep your dialogue authentic!

With members of your cooperative-learning group, present your dialogue in the form of a skit to the entire class.

_____

_____

_____

_____

_____

_____

_____

_____

Spotlight Literary Skill
Point of View

Point of view is the voice that is used to tell the story plot. This story is told by the author using a **third-person narrator.** The author seems to stand outside the story and she refers to all her characters by their names or as he or she. At times she also talks directly to the reader. In Chapter 3, for example, she writes, ''You may imagine the temptation to tell Patrick what happened.''

The events and settings of a story may vary greatly from the point of view of different characters. Choose one scene and describe it from two different points of view. Then draw two sketches to show how the scene would look as seen by each of those two characters. For example, Little Bear's point of view of his experience in the great outdoors might differ from Omri's viewpoint of the same scene.

SCENE: _____ FROM _____'S POINT OF VIEW

_____

_____

_____

_____

_____

SCENE: _____ FROM _____'S POINT OF VIEW

_____

_____

_____

_____

_____

_____'s Point of View   _____'s Point of View

Spotlight Literary Skill
Theme

A **theme** is a central idea in a story. It should not be confused with the series of events, or plot, of a story. One important theme of *The Indian in the Cupboard* is the idea of the importance of friendship. Another theme brought out by the author, Lynne Reid Banks, is the idea that people must accept the responsibility for their actions.

Think about these ideas and then...

1. Find examples of each theme in the story.

2. Tell a personal experience relating to each theme.

Cooperative-Learning Activity
Problem Solving

In this story, Omri encounters many problems. With members of your cooperative-learning group, choose two of Omri's problems. Describe each problem and how Omri solved it. Then tell how you would have solved the problem differently. Be sure to discuss the problem thoroughly within your group. Be prepared to give reasons for your choices.

THE PROBLEM: _____

_____

OMRI'S SOLUTION: _____

_____

_____

OUR SOLUTION: _____

_____

_____

THE PROBLEM: _____

_____

OMRI'S SOLUTION: _____

_____

_____

OUR SOLUTION: _____

_____

_____

Present your solutions to the entire class. Compare your results!

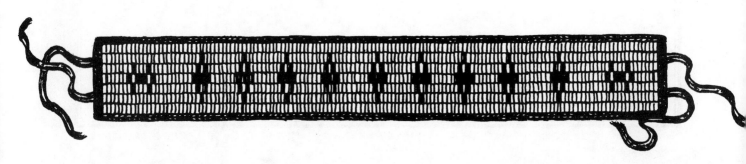

Creative-Writing Activity
Imagine That!

You have just read the fanciful story of Omri, a young boy who possesses a magical time machine in the form of a cupboard that can make any plastic toy come to life. Think about a favorite toy that you had when you were younger. Imagine that this toy had its own real life just like Little Bear or Boone. Describe an adventure that it has when you bring it to life again!

The Magical Adventures of _____

_____

_____

_____

_____

_____

_____

_____

_____

_____

_____

_____

_____

_____

_____

_____

_____

_____

_____

_____

_____

_____

_____

_____

_____

Crossword Puzzle
The Indian in the Cupboard

See how much you remember about *The Indian in the Cupboard*. Have fun!

Across

3. Omri and Little Bear become this.
7. Omri's best friend.
9. Omri has this as a remembrance of Little Bear.
11. English soccer.
14. Gillon's pet.
17. Mr. Johnson.
18. Medical orderly briefly brought to life.
19. The spoken words of the characters (alternate spelling).
20. Accuses Omri of having his gym shorts.
21. Little Bear is from this tribe.

Down

1. British currency unit.
2. Voice used to tell the story.
3. Little Bear's wife.
4. He has artistic talent.
5. The country where the story takes place.
6. One of The Three Sisters.
8. Synonym for *nonplused*.
9. Boone's nickname.
10. Describes this type of story.
12. The author of *The Indian in the Cupboard*.
13. The type of home Little Bear builds.
15. The central idea of a story.
16. Soldiers who fight on horseback.

Post-Reading Activities

1. Learn more about the Iroquois. Make a chart that includes sketches of their shelters, clothing, crafts, and weapons. Draw a map of the geographical areas where they lived. Display your findings on a classroom bulletin board.

2. With your cooperative group, choose a favorite part of the story. Write a script and present your skit to your classmates or to another class.

3. Imagine that you are Omri. Write a diary of your daily thoughts, hopes, and fears. Also record your impressions of other characters.

4. Construct a model longhouse. Use the information given in the pre-reading section and other reference materials to build a replica of the type of longhouse that Little Bear might have had. First, make a sketch of a longhouse and then build your model using as many natural materials as possible.

5. Create a poster to advertise the movie version of the novel. Include information and pictures that will help attract moviegoers!

6. Little Bear was influenced to commit a violent act when he watched a television western. Discuss the ways that cowboys and Native Americans are portrayed in films. Are most honest portrayals or simply stereotypes?

7. Write a different ending to the story!

8. You are there! Suppose you could be a character in the story. Tell which character you would be and how you would change the action.

9. Stage a puppet-show version of the novel. Design your own puppets and stage sets. Present your show to a younger class.

10. What happened next? Lynne Reid Banks has written three sequels to *The Indian in the Cupboard*. Write your own sequel telling what you think happened next in Omri's life or in the life of Boone or Little Bear. Then read one of the author's sequels. Compare it with the original novel.

11. Decide which four characters in the story are most memorable. Your choice may include the characters who came to life. Draw a "photograph" of each of those characters. Above each picture, write the name of the character. Below each picture, write a description of the character.

Glossary of Literary Terms

Alliteration: A repetition of initial, or beginning, sounds in two or more consecutive or neighboring words.

Analogy: A comparison based upon the resemblance in some particular ways between things that are otherwise unlike.

Anecdote: A short account of an interesting, amusing or biographical occurrence.

Anticlimax: An event that is less important than what occurred before it.

Archaic language: Language that was once common in a particular historic period but which is no longer commonly used.

Cause and effect: The relationship in which one condition brings about another condition as a direct result. The result, or consequence, is called the effect.

Character development: The ways in which the author shows how a character changes as the story proceeds.

Characterization: The method used by the author to give readers information about a character; a description or representation of a person's qualities or peculiarities.

Classify: To arrange according to a category or trait.

Climax: The moment when the action in a story reaches its greatest conflict.

Compare and contrast: To examine the likenesses and differences of two people, ideas or things. (*Contrast* always emphasizes differences. *Compare* may focus on likenesses alone or on likenesses and differences.)

Conflict: The main source of drama and tension in a literary work; the discord between persons or forces that brings about dramatic action.

Connotation: Something suggested or implied, not actually stated.

Description: An account that gives the reader a mental image or picture of something.

Dialect: A form of language used in a certain geographic region; it is distinguished from the standard form of the language by pronunciation, grammar and/or vocabulary.

Dialogue (dialog): The parts of a literary work that represent conversation.

Fact: A piece of information that can be proven or verified.

Figurative language: Description of one thing in terms usually used for something else. Simile and metaphor are examples of figurative language.

Flashback: The insertion of an earlier event into the normal chronological sequence of a narrative.

Foreshadowing: The use of clues to give readers a hint of events that will occur later on.

Historical fiction: Fiction represented in a setting true to the history of the time in which the story takes place.

Imagery: Language that appeals to the senses; the use of figures of speech or vivid descriptions to produce mental images.

Irony: The use of words to express the opposite of their literal meaning.

Legend: A story handed down from earlier times; its truth is popularly accepted but cannot be verified.

Limerick: A humorous five-lined poem with a specific form: aabba. Lines 1, 2 and 5 are longer than lines 3 and 4.

Metaphor: A figure of speech that compares two unlike things without the use of like or as.

Mood: The feeling that the author creates for the reader.

Motivation: The reasons for the behavior of a character.

Narrative: The type of writing that tells a story.

Narrator: The character who tells the story.

Opinion: A personal point of view or belief.

Parody: Writing that ridicules or imitates something more serious.

Personification: A figure of speech in which an inanimate object or an abstract idea is given human characteristics.

Play: A literary work that is written in dialogue form and that is usually performed before an audience.

Plot: The arrangement or sequence of events in a story.

Point of view: The perspective from which a story is told.

Protagonist: The main character.

Pun: A play on words that are similar in sound but different in meaning.

Realistic fiction: True-to-life fiction; the people, places and happenings are similar to those in real life.

Resolution: The part of the plot from the climax to the ending where the main dramatic conflict is worked out.

Satire: A literary work that pokes fun at individual or societal weaknesses.

Sequencing: The placement of story elements in the order of their occurrence.

Setting: The time and place in which the story occurs.

Simile: A figure of speech that uses *like* or *as* to compare two unlike things.

Stereotype: A character whose personality traits represent a group rather than an individual.

Suspense: Quality that causes readers to wonder what will happen next.

Symbolism: The use of a thing, character, object or idea to represent something else.

Synonyms: Words that are very similar in meaning.

Tall tale: An exaggerated story detailing unbelievable events.

Theme: The main idea of a literary work; the message the author wants to communicate, sometimes expressed as a generalization about life.

Tone: The quality or feeling conveyed by the work; the author's style or manner of expression.

ANSWERS

Chapter One: Comprehension and Discussion Questions (Answers may vary.)
1. Omri was disappointed because his friend Patrick gave him an old plastic figurine. Omri already had others similar to it and he was getting bored with them.

2. Omri was surprised because he knew that Gillon had no money. When he learned that Gillon had found it in an alley, Omri grew excited because he thought it might be special. Omri loved cupboards because he enjoyed sorting and arranging things inside them.

3. Omri wanted to keep the secret to himself for a while. He was afraid that if he took his eyes off the Indian, the Indian would vanish. Also, he was afraid that his brothers would ridicule him if the Indian was not there.

4. Omri did not laugh at the tiny Indian. Instead, he showed respect and was even a little frightened because the Indian began to act like a real Indian brave.

Chapter Two: Vocabulary

1. excessive	4. astonished	7. eagerly	10. apparently	13. kernel
2. temptation	5. ravenously	8. crestfallen	11. dignified	14. writhed
3. knelt	6. strewn	9. tenderly	12. suspicious	15. row

Chapter Two: Comprehension and Discussion Questions (Answers may vary.)
1. Omri gave "tantalizing hints" to Patrick about the Indian. "Your present was the best thing I got." Although he had wanted a skateboard for weeks, now that he had one, he refused to skate and insisted that he liked the Indian better than the skateboard. He told Patrick that the Indian could speak. Also, he did not invite Patrick to his home.

2. When Omri came home from school and took the Indian out of the cupboard, he found that the Indian had become plastic again. When he put the Indian back into the cupboard, it came to life once again.

3. Omri was very polite and tried hard to please the Indian. He was delighted that Little Bear was still alive.

4. Omri theorized that the Indian would turn to plastic again. Little Bear objected to sleeping in a tepee because the Iroquois slept in a longhouse.

Chapter Three: Vocabulary

1. F	4. N	7. C	10. G	13. K
2. A	5. J	8. D	11. O	14. H
3. L	6. B	9. E	12. I	15. M

Chapter Three: Comprehension and Discussion Questions (Answers may vary.)
1. Omri was excited and happy because when he put the plastic tepee in the cupboard and used the key, the tepee became real. In contrast, Little Bear was not happy. He refused to use the tepee because it did not have Iroquois signs on it. He said the tepee was "no good" for an Iroquois. Also, he took the magic for granted. "So? Magic. The spirits work much magic."

2. Little Bear was beginning to trust Omri. He believed Omri's promise not to hold him too tightly.

3. He learned that Little Bear was a real person who had lived long ago and had killed many men. He had fought with the English against the French during the French and Indian Wars. He had taken scalps. Omri tried to justify Little Bear's actions by comparing them to modern warfare.

4. Omri thought that Little Bear and the horse might ride away and be attacked by an animal.

Chapters Four and Five: Vocabulary

1. unwilling	3. cliff	5. deal	7. bandage	9. show fear	11. complex
2. relatives	4. cringing	6. jacket	8. positive	10. . . .vessel	12. abandoned

Chapter Four: Comprehension and Discussion Questions (Answers may vary.)
1. When his father scolded him, Omri accidentally tightened his hold on the box that contained Little Bear and the horse.

2. Omri spied a plastic World War I medical orderly in his toy collection. He hoped to use the soldier's medical bag to care for Little Bear's wound.

Chapter Five: Comprehension and Discussion Questions (Answers may vary.)
1. Omri told Tommy that he was just having a dream.

2. Answers will vary, but Little Bear and Tommy were real people from different time periods. Omri thought they might not get along. Omri had his hands full just meeting Little Bear's needs.

Chapter Six: Comprehension and Discussion Questions (Answers may vary.)
1. Omri wanted to find out more about the Iroquois so that he would understand Little Bear better and would learn more about his life.

2. Maize (corn), squash, and beans were the mainstays of the Iroquois diet.

3. Omri did not like knights, so he did not mind grabbing the ax. In Chapter 5 we were told that "Omri had very little time for knights." He thought of them as murderers. He had sympathy for the old chief, however, and tried to treat him gently.

4. Answers will vary.

Chapter Seven: Vocabulary
Answers will vary, but a possible synonym/antonym is given for each:

1. esteem/disapproval	6. weak/strong	11. ridiculing/praising
2. affliction/pleasure	7. stimulate/discourage	12. respectfully/disrespectfully
3. disorder/order	8. stare/ignore	13. seriously/frivolously
4. concede/remain steadfast	9. skeptical/gullible	14. alcoholic/non-alcoholic
5. overwhelm/abandon	10. forgiving/unforgiving	15. eerie/natural

Chapter Seven: Comprehension and Discussion (Answers may vary.)

1. Omri valued Patrick's friendship. He believed that if he didn't tell his secret to his friend, their friendship might be over. Omri also longed for the thrill of showing someone else the magical feat.

2. Omri thought that his brothers had seen Little Bear. Instead, they were looking at Gillon's rat and the longhouse. Omri told them that the sound they heard was just a clockwork dolphin under his bed.

3. Answers will vary.

4. Answers will vary.

Chapter Eight: Vocabulary

1. doggedly	3. heron	5. spellbound	7. dune	9. mulish	11. index	13. embedded
2. enormous	4. buckskin	6. savory	8. infinite	10. aghast	12. instinctive	14. abrupt

MESSAGE: Do you believe in magic? Omri does.

Chapter Eight: Comprehension and Discussion (Answers may vary.)

1. Omri and Patrick argued because Omri did not want Patrick to have a live person of his own.

2. When Little Bear's food was accidentally ruined, Omri went downstairs to get him more food. It was an error in judgment because he left Patrick alone with the cupboard, the key, and the plastic figurines.

3. Among the Iroquois, it was the custom for a man's mother to find a suitable wife for him. Because Little Bear's mother was not available, Little Bear wanted Omri to act like his mother and find him a wife!

4. Omri was upset that Patrick threatened to reveal the secret of the little people; however, because the boys were such close friends and Omri didn't want to lose the friendship, Omri agreed to bring the little people to school the next day.

Chapter Nine: Vocabulary

1. infuriated	3. tethered	5. frenzied	7. offended	9. gleeful	11. relish	13. varmint
2. scornfully	4. coaxed	6. Tactics	8. peered	10. makeshift	12. prostrate	14. mime

Chapter Nine: Comprehension and Discussion Questions (Answers may vary.)

1. The cowboy thought he was having hallucinations caused by drinking too much liquor.

2. The horses had smelled each other, and the cowboy and his horse had escaped through a knot in the wall of the wooden crate.

3. Omri threatened not to bring him a wife if he killed the cowboy.

4. Boone's nickname was Boohoo. He got it because he cried so easily.

Chapter Ten: Comprehension and Discussion Questions (Answers may vary.)

1. Omri told them that they wouldn't get any breakfast unless they declared a truce while they ate.

2. Omri seemed rather unskilled. He dropped shell in the egg; the egg wasn't cooked in the center; and the beans were cold. Little Bear and Boone seemed to be satisfied, however, for they ate heartily.

3. Boone was trying to put off the inevitable fight with Little Bear.

4. It was time to go to school. Omri would have ended it sooner if he had thought they would seriously harm one another. "Omri was ready to part them" as soon as they began to fight.

Chapter Eleven: Vocabulary

1. M	4. H	7. K	10. B	13. O	16. F
2. E	5. P	8. A	11. G	14. J	17. L
3. D	6. I	9. C	12. Q	15. N	

Chapter Eleven: Comprehension and Discussion Questions (Answers may vary.)

1. He said that without the dust and sweat, his clothes wouldn't keep him warm.

2. Answers will vary.

3. Little Bear wanted Omri to put Boone in the same pocket because he was lonely.

4. Answers will vary.

Chapter Twelve: Vocabulary

1. expectation	3. equipment	5. closed	7. scented	9. gesture
2. inclined	4. strike	6. hesitated	8. nervously	

Possible synonyms are:

1. principal	3. ask	5. sullenly	7. maximum
2. uncontrollable	4. appeared	6. disheveled	8. ordinary

Chapter Twelve: Comprehension and Discussion Questions (Answers may vary.)

1. Answers will vary.

2. Patrick had been pushed onto the floor, and Omri started to imagine that terrible things had happened to the little men. He tried to get hold of himself and to stop jumping to conclusions.

3. Omri treated Little Bear with respect and dignity—as if he were a real person. Patrick treated Boone like a toy.

4. Mr. Johnson's face had turned white and his mouth was hanging open. Patrick was crying.

Chapter Thirteen: Comprehension and Discussion Questions (Answers may vary.)

1. He wanted to keep his promise, but he realized that it would be another "live little person to worry about."

2. Omri learned that Boone was an excellent artist.

3. Answers will vary, but in this chapter it was revealed that Boone was an excellent artist, and Omri was accused of shoplifting.

4. Patrick came to Omri's defense when the shopkeeper accused Omri of stealing the two figures. Omri then invited him to stay overnight to witness the bringing to life of Little Bear's wife.

Chapter Fourteen: Comprehension and Discussion (Answers may vary.)

1. Adiel had taken Omri's cupboard because he wrongly believed that Omri had taken his football (soccer) shorts. Omri knew that he couldn't win a physical confrontation with Ariel because Ariel was much larger.

2. He wanted Little Bear to be happy. Without the key, Little Bear and Boone would be destined to remain two little men in a land of "giants."

3. "Omri was too ashamed to admit he'd lost the key she'd told him to be so careful of."

4. Little Bear seemed to regret it. He said, "Little Bear sorry." He suggested they get the doctor back. When Omri explained that that was impossible, Little Bear removed the arrow and tended the wound. Little Bear sobbed.

Chapter Fifteen: Vocabulary

1. H	3. E	5. I	7. L	9. F	11. D
2. K	4. G	6. B	8. J	10. C	12. A

Chapter Fifteen: Comprehension and Discussion (Answers may vary.)

1. Only Little Bear was small enough to get to the other side of the wooden wall where Omri believed the key had dropped. They needed the key to bring the plastic doctor to life to help Boone. Omri had forgotten about the rat and he feared for Little Bear's life when he remembered.

2. These things had not yet been discovered during Tommy's lifetime.

3. Little Bear wanted to do a dance to get the spirits to let Boone live. He was willing to risk his safety by going under the floor. He didn't deny being Boone's pal when asked by Tommy. He accepted the responsibility of giving Boone his medication. Also, he agreed to make Boone his blood brother.

4. When Boone came to, he asked about the picture they had been watching on TV. He insulted the Indians, calling them savages.

Chapter Sixteen: Vocabulary

1. bewildered	3. stressful	5. relapse	7. chanting	9. nick	11. swabbed
2. lingered	4. flourish	6. pommel	8. stealthily	10. fate

Chapter Sixteen: Comprehension and Discussion Questions (Answers may vary.)

1. He was concerned about what would happen when he brought the woman to life. He wanted to keep Little Bear, but he knew that wouldn't be possible. All of the scenarios he played out in his mind had ended in disaster.

2. Answers will vary, but she was bewildered enough. She would probably have been frightened by such a "giant."

3. They became blood brothers.

4. Omri had Little Bear's belt. Little Bear had given it to Omri as payment for his wife.

Spotlight Literary Skill: Theme (Answers may vary.)

Answers will vary, but the following are possible examples.

Theme 1: Omri realized that his friendship with Patrick was valuable. It might be over if he did not share the secret of the Indian with his friend. Omri decided to tell Patrick the truth.

Theme 2: Omri realized that he could not adequately care for the little people that he had brought to life. He learned that it was an awesome responsibility because he had to treat them as real people and not as toys. He finally decided to return them to their original existence.

Crossword Puzzle

© **1996 Educational Impressions, Inc.**